MEET BETTER

167 Easy Ways
to Make Your Events More
Environmentally and **Socially Responsible**

Mariela McIlwraith, CMP, CMM, MBA
Shawna McKinley, MAEEC
Nancy J. Zavada, CMP

Published by MeetGreen®
Portland, OR, USA
May, 2015

Printed on 55% post-consumer recycled content paper using low VOC, vegetable based inks.

Library of Congress Control Number: 2015907633

Printed in the United States of America.

ISBN: 978-0-9835975-1-3

CONTENTS

LETTER TO OUR READERS

Dear Reader,

In recent years, we've seen a great evolution towards sustainability in the meetings and events industry. It's been exciting to be a part of it, even though it has taken us in unexpected directions. When we first started out as event professionals we envisioned going to galas, not dumpster diving. We thought we'd be admiring the chandeliers, not asking about the light bulbs. We thought that our concern at banquets would be waist management, not waste management. All of this has given us some good insights and practical know-how that we want to share with you to help you get started in sustainable events.

This book is all about getting started. These are the easy, low-hanging fruit to make your event more environmentally and socially responsible. This book is not intended to be all-encompassing, but it is intended to help you to take your first step (or 167 first steps). Hopefully, it will help spark an excitement for sustainable events that will encourage you to continue on the path.

This book has three sections: the first considers how to integrate sustainability into the core elements of meeting planning and covers the logistical aspects of planning an event. From there, we consider how program elements can reflect sustainability. We wrap up with a next steps section that is all about helping you to take sustainability further in your events and organizations.

THIS BOOK IS FOR YOU IF YOU ARE:

✔ **Looking for demystified, practical advice about sustainable events**

✔ **Excited about sustainable events and need a place to start**

✔ **Wanting to make your organization an industry leader**

✔ **Assigned to "green our meetings" and need a roadmap**

✔ **Looking for new ways to attract event sponsors**

✔ **Needing to find new cost savings opportunities**

✔ **Wanting to engage with your event participants in a new way**

✔ **Wanting to expand your skills as an event professional**

✔ **Wanting to reduce the environmental footprint of your event**

✔ **Wanting to give back to the community**

✔ **Wanting to impress your boss or clients with your achievements**

✔ **Wanting to take meeting design to the next level**

Thank you for reading!

Mariela, Shawna and Nancy

WHY WE DO WHAT WE DO

As we polished off the book, we reached out to some of our trusted friends and partners and asked them how sustainable practices have affected them and how we can keep the momentum going. Here is what they had to say:

With the world's marine life quickly being depleted, it is essential that we start making more responsible choices when it comes to seafood. Simple choices, such as including sustainable seafood options at your next event, will help ensure the health of our oceans for generations to come.

Vancouver Aquarium's Ocean Wise™ program (www.oceanwise.ca)

Destined to be a must read for all meeting professionals, *Meet Better* offers planners 167 reasons to think sustainability first and foremost with their events. Our industry still does a very poor job of redirecting excess resources, such as food, to those who need it most. With an estimated 50 million people in the US living in food insecure households, we need to think first how to properly re-purpose the excess food (as well as all other sustainability components) at our events. Whether it's using tech tools to help green an event, or understanding how much impact our meeting selections have on our environment, Mariela, Shawna and Nancy are to be commended for this thorough review of how to reduce our carbon (CO_2e) footprint on this planet directly through our industry. With our industry's excesses, all meeting professionals need to get on this sustainability train now. Here's your ticket as to how to do it!

James Spellos, CMP, President, Meeting U. (www.meeting-u.com)

Events help local economies, build business, and relationships. But bringing groups together also impacts the environment, and contributes to climate change. More and more event planners, hosts, and attendees are taking responsibility for their impact by reducing emissions and implementing offset programs to bridge the gap to net zero impact. Carbon offsets address emissions that are impossible to reduce by using funds to help eliminate emissions elsewhere. Carbon offset projects can invest in alternative, cleaner and renewable energy sources, such as wind power, farm power and landfill gas capture. They can be integrated into events in a variety of ways, through sponsorship, attendee opt-ins in registration or as a budget expense. With the cost being much less than you might think, carbon offsets are an easy way for planners to make a significant difference and help build a better energy future.

Nancy Bsales, Manager, Carbon Solutions, TerraPass (www.terrapass.com)

As we move into a new age of enlightenment regarding food waste and recovery, a comprehensive sustainable event guide has never been more needed. Rock and Wrap It Up! works with event planners to find suitable agencies who will recover food from conference locations throughout North America. Our Whole Earth Calculator mobile app converts pounds of food into total meals and GHG reduction stats that planners can share with participants via social media. Even a small donation of 100 pounds can prepare 77 meals, showing the important difference an event professional can make through food recovery.

Syd Mandelbaum, Rock and Wrap it Up CEO (rockandwrapitup.org)

ACKNOWLEDGMENTS

FROM ALL OF US:

We are grateful to our expert reviewers who provided important feedback on the book including Scott Craighead, Joan Eisenstodt, Lawrence Leonard, Janet Sperstad, Andrew Walker and Sandra Wood. We absolutely could not have produced this without the amazing talents (and patience!) of our graphic designer, Erika Abrams and research support from Aaron Elliott. We were also fortunate to have support from industry leaders who pre-ordered copies of the book. These early adopters helped make it possible for us to make the best choices for environmentally responsible printing. This included:

- BizBash
- Convention Industry Council
- Destination Marketing Association International's empowerMINT.com
- Fairmont Washington, D.C., Georgetown
- IMEX
- International Association of Exhibitions and Events
- QuickMobile
- Semiahmoo Resort
- Tourism Toronto
- Vancouver Convention Centre

FROM MARIELA:

First, thanks to Shawna and Nancy for saying yes to working on this! I've never had a more informative card game than the one we played over a weekend in Vancouver sharing our sustainable event tips. Thanks as well to my family, especially Thomas and Allie for reading *The Lorax* with me and reminding me, as Dr. Seuss wrote, "Unless someone like you cares a whole awful lot, nothing is going to get better. It's not." Thanks as well to Tad for being supportive when I told him I was taking on another book project, and for talking me through moments of writer's block.

FROM SHAWNA:

Thanks to Tracy London, Russell Clark and Kitty Ratcliffe who almost two decades ago agreed to support a naive university student in creating an online resource center for green meetings. Our list of tips was much shorter then, and it's been an inspiring journey to expand it by working with many dedicated students, clients, and peers in the years since, especially Nancy and Mariela. Much love to Dad and Mom for sparking a steward by taking me outside, and my ever-patient Brad who encourages me in all things I do.

FROM NANCY:

Without the heroic efforts of everyday champions in host organizations, event venues, catering companies, general decorators, recycling companies, volunteers, hotels, and others, meeting more sustainably would have fallen away as a short-lived trend. Instead, it is here to stay. To those good humans doing the "hard work," this book is for you. I have learned from and been inspired by each of you. For my biggest fan, Bob, who believes in me, my work and that love (for each other and the planet) is ultimately the answer.

PART ONE:
CORE ELEMENTS

 **Food and Beverage Planning**

 **Food and Beverage Service**

 **Site Selection**

 **Waste Management**

 **Transportation and Travel**

 **Purchasing Practices**

 **Onsite Management**

FOOD *and* BEVERAGE PLANNING

1. **Donate leftover food.**
   Some venues or caterers may have concerns about liability, however, many laws protect food donors. Contact the food bank to confirm local regulations and practice safe food handling.

2. **Serve seasonal food from local farms and vendors.**
   Buying locally supports the community's economy and typically results in fresher food. It also helps to reduce your food miles, though this is only one factor in determining the environmental impact of your menus. 83 percent of the average US household's carbon footprint for food comes from growing and producing it. Transportation is only 11 percent.[1]

3. **Be flexible and allow the chef to make decisions that meet your budget and sustainability goals.**

4. **Ask your chef to minimize air-freighted food.**
   Pay particular attention to fish and tropical fruit. These can significantly increase the carbon footprint of your menu.

5. **Carefully order food to minimize waste.**
   Very often, event planners guarantee numbers across the board for all functions. Instead, cross-check with arrival and departures and past history to make adjustments for each meal function.

6. **Make food and scheduling choices that consider health, faith and values of participants.**
   As meeting and event professionals, part of our work involves creating environments that are welcoming to all participants. Anticipating and preparing for your participant's needs, whether they be for healthy options, menus that meet faith requirements or offering alternatives such as vegetarian menus will go a long way to creating this welcoming environment. Also consider reducing the number of courses from four to three, and serving smaller portions.

7. **Create sustainable menu themes such as Meatless Monday, or a Blemished Buffet.**
   High quality food is often discarded for being imperfectly shaped or blemished. In 2013, the United Nations chose to highlight this issue by serving a five-course meal made from food that was considered to be reject-grade by the standards of European buyers. The event was for 500 delegates at a week-long United Nations Environment Programme (UNEP) event in Kenya.[2]

8. **Ensure all seafood meets requirements of a program such as Seafood Watch, Vancouver Aquarium's Ocean Wise, or the Marine Stewardship Council.**
   It's important to reconfirm sustainable choices close to the event date as the ratings can change due to stock levels.

9. **Choose chicken or vegetarian instead of beef.**
   Different foods have different water and carbon footprints. It can take over three times as much water to raise one kilogram of beef compared to one kilogram of chicken.[3]

10. **Serve fairly-traded coffee, tea and chocolate.**

11. **Make meat choices that are more sustainable such as grass fed, no antibiotics or hormones, certified organic and/or humane, cage free and free range.**

WHERE DOES YOUR FOOD
COME FROM?

CERTIFIED ORGANIC

Certified organic foods are grown and processed according to federal guidelines addressing factors such as soil quality, animal raising practices, pest and weed control and the use of biologically based farming methods. Look for assurance by USDA, QA, or a reputable verifier in your region.

NATURAL

In some regions, including Canada and the US, there are guidelines for the use of the term "natural" that include requirements for minimal processing and no added ingredients. However, it can mean a number of different things and does not provide assurances.

FREE RANGE OR FREE ROAMING

Free range animals have access to the outdoors at least part of the day. This term may mean different things depending on prevailing standards.

FREE RUN

Allowed to run freely in an indoor area and not kept in cages.

ANTIBIOTIC FREE

Meat or poultry must have sufficient documentation provided by the producer to the local verifying authority (such as the USDA) demonstrating the animals were raised without antibiotics.

CHEMICAL FREE

Food or drink free from or produced without the use of artificial chemicals.

FAIRLY TRADED

Small farmers are paid a fair market price that enables them to improve their standard of living.

GMO-FREE FOODS

Foods that do not include genetically modified organisms.

"IF YOU CAN'T PRONOUNCE THE INGREDIENTS, DON'T EAT IT."

—*Common Sense*

Sustainable SEAFOOD

Seafood can be a healthy and sustainable menu option for events. Choose seafood that has received a positive rating by organizations such as Seafood Watch (US), Ocean Wise (Canada) or Marine Stewardship Council (UK).

ISSUES TO WATCH

DISCARDS AND BYCATCH
According to the UN's Food and Agriculture Organization, there is an estimated 7.3 million metric tons of annual fisheries discards.[4] This includes non-target species (bycatch) and discarded target species. To minimize bycatch, look for selective harvesting practices such as harpooning, pole and line, jigging and setting traps or pots. Also look for dolphin friendly certification for tuna.

FOOD CHAIN DISRUPTION
Substantially affecting populations of top predators can be very disruptive to an ecosystem. Top predators also tend to have higher mercury levels.

OVERFISHING
Many species are being caught at rates higher than they can be replaced through natural reproduction. According to the World Wildlife Federation, more than 85 percent of the world's fisheries have been pushed to or beyond their biological limits and are in need of strict management plans to restore them.[5]

HARVEST METHOD
Some fishing methods can be destructive, but most have alternatives that are more sustainable. Methods of greatest concern for damage to the seafloor include bottom trawling and dredging. These two methods, as well as gillnetting, can also result in high levels of bycatch.

FISH FARMING METHOD
When done right, farmed fish can be a very sustainable option. Watch for best practices in fish farming including closed containment to avoid concerns about contaminating wild stocks and waste water management. Farmed fish should also provide net protein gains by using less wild fish as feed than it produces. Open net and submersible net pens should be avoided.

SHELLFISH FARMING METHOD
Oysters, mussels and clams are filter feeders, meaning that they don't need additional feed in order to grow. Shellfish culture can be sustainable provided that it is done in tidal areas to avoid waste accumulation and non-native species introduction is avoided.

5 TIPS FOR SUSTAINABLE SEAFOOD:

1 **Trash Fish Dinners:** Since 2013, the Chef's Collaborative in the US has been hosting trash fish dinners to highlight lesser known-species of fish, thereby reducing pressure on overfished species and helping local fishing communities.[6]

2 **Get the App:** Download a sustainable seafood app for your area. Check it close to your event date since recommendations can fluctuate seasonally.

3 **Local and Seasonal:** Your seafood's carbon footprint increases significantly with airfreight. Choose local and seasonal seafood whenever possible.

4 **Fish Fridays:** Ask your venue to offer a Fish Friday menu to all their in-house groups (known as ganging menus). The more groups using the same menu, the better for managing food waste. For added impact, leave the menu flexible, allowing your chef to make adjustments for the most sustainable option in your budget.

5 **Shark Fin Free Events:** Demand for shark fins is resulting in high harvesting levels of this top predator. They are typically used for shark fin soup, a highly valued delicacy that represents status and generosity. Instead, offer an alternative menu item or gift to replace not only the shark fin as an ingredient, but also the symbolism associated with it.

Food for Thought:

Since shellfish is a common allergen and has faith-based restrictions, remember to offer alternatives if you have shellfish on the menu. Also confirm that safe food handling is followed to avoid cross-contamination.

12. **Do not refresh break services and buffets until they are close to empty.**
Some caterers refresh with 5 percent of food remaining, so it helps to ask what the norm is. If food can be held in a nearby kitchen or hot-box you may be safe to reduce to 1 percent or less. Towards the end of the function, ask for smaller refresh amounts.

13. **Serve food in reusable containers or service ware.**

14. **Serve condiments in bulk.**
Sugar, milk and cream, mustard, ketchup, dressings and sauces can all be served in bulk instead of in individual containers that increase waste. Address hygiene and safety concerns by using pumps, covered, enclosed and pour containers.

15. **Banish individual disposable plastic water bottles.**
Instead, offer water stations.

16. **Change from filtered to tap water if water is potable.**
These can be flavored with slices of fresh citrus, cucumber, herbs or berries for added interest.

17. **Order bulk lemonade, flavored waters and iced tea instead of individually packaged sodas.**

18. **Avoid presetting food (such as salads and desserts) to help minimize waste.**
Alternatively, only preset 80 percent of the tables and have the rest served as needed.

19. **Do not pre-fill water glasses at banquets.**

20. **Reduce plate sizes.**
In 2012, Nordic Choice Hotels, in cooperation with GreeNudge and CICERO conducted a food waste study. Hotels with smaller plates reduced food waste by 19.5 percent and those with information signs reduced it by 20.5 percent without affecting guest satisfaction. When implemented at all their hotels, smaller plates would result in 556 metric tons of food waste avoided annually and 31 billion Norwegian kroner saved.[7]

21. **Avoid air-freighted or greenhouse grown flowers.**
Live, local, in-season flowers can add a beautiful touch to décor. Alternatively, ask your chef for recommendations for pots of fresh herbs that complement the meals and that can be used by guests to select their favorite garnish.

22. **Make sure centerpieces are reusable or can be donated.**
You can also make them available to your guests or volunteers to take home, or arrange a draw for them at the end of the event.

23. **Reduce pre-packaging or allow "build-your-own" lunchboxes to reduce food waste.**

CHECK OUT THE "LOVE FOOD, HATE WASTE" WEBSITE FOR MORE IDEAS.
www.lovefoodhatewaste.com

Food Service Ware Guide

A 5,000 PERSON CONVENTION *uses*

45,000 CUPS

35,000 PLATES

15,000 CUTLERY SETS

Over **3 DAYS**

REDUCE YOUR FOOTPRINT with *sustainable serviceware options:*

Polystyrene — Recyclable plastic — Compostable paper, plastic, wood — Reusable service ware

LESS SUSTAINABLE → **MORE SUSTAINABLE**

CUPPA CONUNDRUM?

In a study of 2,000 uses, **ceramic mugs were the lowest-carbon choice,** followed by foam and paper.[8]

BUYING COMPOSTABLE? LOOK FOR:

BPI Compostable (ASTM D6400/ASTM D6868)

OK Compost

24. **Use a green building as your venue.**
Keep an eye out for programs to reduce waste (composting and recycling), energy (efficient bulbs and occupancy sensors), and water (low flow faucets, toilets and showers). Alternatively, look for LEED® certified buildings.

25. **Use a green hotel for guest rooms.**
Check for third party certification such as Green Key, Green Seal, EarthCheck, ISO 14001, APEX/ ASTM Environmentally Sustainable Event Standards and LEED®.

26. **Select accessible venues.**
Ask for verification of compliance with regulations related to accessibility. In the US, ask for proof of compliance with ADA (Americans with Disabilities Act) regulations. In other countries, confirm if regulations are federal, state/provincial/regional or municipal and verify compliance.

27. **Ask the Destination Management Organization (DMO) / Convention and Visitors Bureau (CVB) for a list of green vendors including local talent, artisans, restaurants, shopping, décor, etc.**

28. **Make sure hotel rooms have a linen reuse program that they actively honour.**

29. **Request recycling bins in guest rooms.**
One hotel used specially-marked brown paper bags to pilot the program before going to the expense of bins. It was such a success, they invested!

30. **Select a hotel with guest amenity dispenser for soap and shampoo.**
Alternatively, ask if they participate in a donation program for partially used amenities, or ask participants to bring their own soap and shampoo.

31. **Request in-room coffee service with no polystyrene cups or single-serve pods.**
Single serve coffee pods can cost $50 USD per pound, and create a lot of landfill.[9]

32. **Consider airlift to destination and proximity to participants.**
If possible, choose a site that minimizes air travel for participants.

33. **Select venues in close proximity to each other to encourage walking.**

34. **Ask your venue if they use renewable energy sources.**
Renewable energy sources may include wind, solar, hydro and geothermal.

35. **Ensure that non-smoking space is available and designated smoking areas have air filtration and ashtrays.**

36. **Look for existing building features such as digital signage, rigging points, greenery, natural lighting and carpeted expo space that will make it easier to use sustainable materials.**

37. **Ensure the venue uses environmentally-friendly cleaning supplies and confirm that staff is properly trained in their use.**
This may include Green Seal or EcoLogo certified products.

Best Practices for SITE SELECTION

Selecting a site that helps you to meet your sustainability goals is one of the most important steps towards making your event more socially and environmentally responsible.

BEST PRACTICES TO WATCH FOR

	PEOPLE	**WATER**	**WASTE**	**ENERGY**
Hotel Guest Rooms	• Training in identifying and reporting human trafficking	• Linen and towel reuse programs	• Bulk amenity dispensers • Amenity donation program	• Occupancy or key card sensors
All event spaces	• Accessible • Anti-harassment policy • Health and safety records • Diversity and inclusion policy	• Low flow fixtures • Water smart landscaping and grounds maintenance	• Recycling • Composting • Donation program for food, event materials and other goods	• Efficient lighting • Sensor-activated HVAC system • Green energy purchasing and carbon offsets

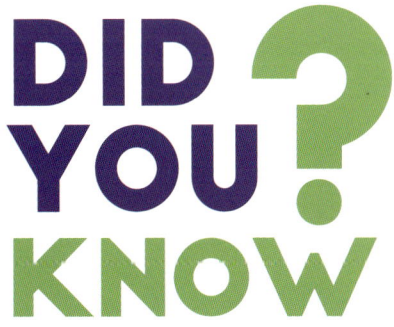

DID YOU KNOW?

Clean the World is a charitable organization that collects, sanitizes and distributes used hotel amenities (such as soap) to help fight hygiene related illnesses around the world. As of April 2015, Clean the World has distributed more than 22 million bars of soap in 96 countries.[10]

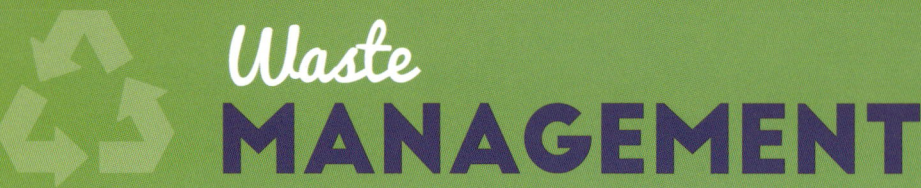

Waste MANAGEMENT

38. **Implement a recycling program both front and back of house.**
Remember even if your venue does the sorting for you, participants will be reassured if they see it happening.

39. **Hire or appoint a waste coordinator for your event.**

40. **Research local food donation regulations and educate vendors.**

41. **Donate food and/or compost food waste.**
Researching local regulations will help you anticipate liability concerns vendors may have.

42. **Select a destination that has commercial composting and recycling in place.**
This will set you up for success from the outset, reduce costs for a waste program and make your sustainability program much easier to implement.

43. **Donate leftover exhibit materials to organizations such as Habitat for Humanity, RePurpose America or school and artist supply houses.**

44. **Ask for bins in meeting rooms and clearly label all waste bins.**
Remember attendees may be used to different recycling procedures in their hometown, and may not speak the local language. Clear pictures and color-coded waste bins help!

45. **Ask the venue to measure your waste.**
It's best to ask for measurement in advance, as not all venues regularly track waste on a per event basis. Hotel venues may offer free event footprint measurement if it is requested before the event.

46. **Ask event technology vendors to donate or recycle their batteries, cables and equipment.**

THE TYPICAL **CONVENTION ATTENDEE** PRODUCES **2.5KG** OF WASTE PER DAY **1.0KG** OF WHICH IS LANDFILL[11]

FOR A **2-DAY, 1000 PERSON EVENT** THIS ADDS UP TO **5 METRIC TONS OF WASTE** *and* **2 METRIC TONS** OF LANDFILL

WASTE AUDITS REVEAL THIS CAN INCLUDE[12]

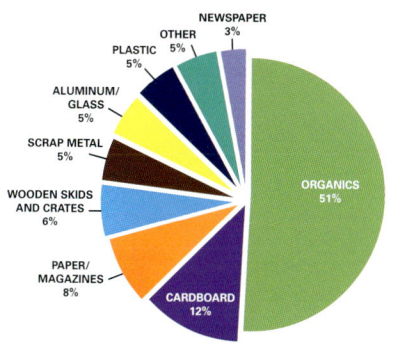

HOTEL MEETING (NO TRADE SHOW)

- NEWSPAPER 3%
- OTHER 5%
- PLASTIC 5%
- ALUMINUM/GLASS 5%
- SCRAP METAL 5%
- WOODEN SKIDS AND CRATES 6%
- PAPER/MAGAZINES 8%
- CARDBOARD 12%
- ORGANICS 51%

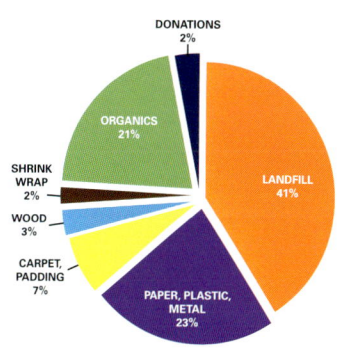

CONVENTION TRADE SHOW EVENT

- DONATIONS 2%
- ORGANICS 21%
- SHRINK WRAP 2%
- WOOD 3%
- CARPET, PADDING 7%
- PAPER, PLASTIC, METAL 23%
- LANDFILL 41%

Four steps TO LESS WASTE

1 REDUCE AT SOURCE: Food waste costs $165 billion per year in the US, so check your guarantees![13]

2 REUSE: Renting used carpet saves 1.9 kg (4.2 lbs) of landfill per square yard.[14]

3 RECYCLE AND COMPOST: Recycling employs 1.1 million people in the USA, earning $236 billion in gross revenues each year.[15]

4 DONATE: 250 pounds of donated food creates 192 meals for those in need.[16]

47. **Plan an area for no-idling of motor coaches with a sponsored lounge for waiting.**
Many cities will have a no-idling ordinance. Ensure that the law is observed or if there is no local law, establish a no-idling policy for your event.

48. **Encourage participants to offset their event footprint.**
This includes staff and participant travel and exhibitor freight, as well as venue and hotel energy use. Carbon offsets help us be accountable for the emissions impacts we can't avoid, such as those from air travel. By paying for an offset, participants can invest in various projects that prevent emissions equal to their impact. This may include wind power, tree planting or energy efficiency programs. Offsets can be embedded in your registration fee, or offered as an optional package in registration systems.

49. **Use shuttles with pre-set schedules to reduce waiting and run full loads.**

50. **Reduce single vehicle trips.**
Promote carpooling, car sharing, public transit, and provide incentives to use these such as a transit pass discount, free parking for carpool cars and designated driver programs.

51. **Promote rail transport for attendees with incentives for use, such as reduced fees.**

52. **Use a transit ambassador at the airport to encourage use of mass transit.**
In San Francisco, a round trip to and from the airport by light rapid transit can eliminate 9 kg (20 pounds) of emissions, and saves attendees $60 USD compared to using a taxi![17]

53. **Use modern and efficient buses and car service.**
One way to screen for more efficient buses is to ask about the age of the buses you'll be booking. Newer coaches will typically have more fuel-efficient, cleaner-burning engines.

54. **Take advantage of destination bike loan programs.**

How much carbon is that?
FIND OUT FUN METAPHORS FOR CARBON METRICS AT
www.epa.gov/cleanenergy/ energy-resources/calculator.html

What is a CO2e?

The carbon footprint of an event or meeting can contribute significantly to climate change. Carbon dioxide equivalent (CO2e) is a standard measure used for carbon footprints. It combines all of the greenhouse gas emissions for a product or service and converts them into a standard unit, making it easier to compare different choices. As an example, it takes 10g of CO2 equivalents to fill an average party balloon.[18]

EXAMPLE	CARBON DIOXIDE EQUIVALENTS	BALLOON EQUIVALENT
London 2012 Olympics (with a strong sustainability program)	3.3 million metric tons of CO2e[19]	330,000,000,000
Typical conference attendee (per day)	177 kg (390 pounds)[20]	17,700
Travel options (Washington, DC to New York City – 232 miles/373 kilometres):		
• Air (short haul)	67.14 kg	6,714
• Rail (passenger)	22.38 kg	2,238
• Car (average petrol)	74.6 kg	7,460[21]

Purchasing PRACTICES

55. **Buy materials made from recycled content.**
This may include lanyards, badges, bags, paper and carpet.

56. **Identify, reduce and eliminate polyvinyl chloride (PVC).**
PVC is often found in tabletops, banners and name badge holders.

57. **Hire businesses that further a social purpose and give back to communities such as inner city skills training and youth programs.**

58. **Avoid the use of decal and adhesive signs, which typically end up in landfill.**

59. **Reduce and eliminate plastic film as it can be difficult to recycle.**

60. **Pre-plan materials to reduce volume of waste.**

61. **Eliminate conference bags or ask on the registration form if they require one.**
See Sponsor section for alternative revenue sources.

62. **Print one-time signage on recyclable material such as cardboard.**

63. **Ask your event technology provider to use the most efficient lights, sound and projection equipment available to achieve the desired experience.**

64. **Ask your promotional product provider if items are sourced from factories that don't use forced and child labor and have health and safety records.**

65. **Use upcycled products and upcycle your stuff.**
Upcycling is the use of materials that would otherwise be discarded to make new products. An example would be to produce conference bags from banners used at your last event.

66. **Ask your vendor to provide verification that their products do not contain harmful chemicals.**
This may include BPA, and formaldehyde (commonly found in textiles and fiberboard).

67. **Banish polystyrene, typically known as Styrofoam.**

68. **Replace name badge holders with a name card only.**

69. **Avoid manufacturing waste.**
Use flat faced instead of curved design for builds, reducing the need for PVC products and eliminating unusable trim pieces for kiosks and flooring in the exhibit hall.

STUMPED BY
SUSTAINABILITY SLANG?

Here's our layperson's guide to 10 common green marketing terms

RECYCLED CONTENT	Event stuff that is made from other stuff that was used before. Perhaps by a manufacturer (post-industrial) or a consumer (post-consumer).	Most trade show vendors can provide post-industrial recycled content carpet and padding if asked.
RECYCLABLE	Material that can be re-processed into something else if disposed of properly.	Cardboard is recyclable by most venues. Certain plastics, carpet and metals may need special handling to be recycled properly.
BIODEGRADABLE	This stuff may break down and is designed to be landfilled.	Always ask for proof of testing for any product marketed as biodegradable, such as name badges.
COMPOSTABLE	A special kind of biodegradation, where material is tested to break-down into specific compounds at a certain rate in a commercial facility.	To make sure your food service ware is compostable, ask if it is tested to comply with ASTM D6400, ASTM D6868, or EN 13432.
RENEWABLE ENERGY	Forget coal, oil and fossil fuels. This stuff is powered by wind, solar, hydro or biomass.	Venues can have renewable energy onsite, such as solar panels, or they may purchase utility-generated renewable power.
FAIR LABOR	People who made this stuff receive a living wage and work in a safe and healthy environment.	Look for fairly traded labels on things like flowers, produce, coffee and chocolate. Also ask if factories producing promotional products are inspected for safe conditions.
LOCAL	We bought this nearby. Rule of thumb: within 250 miles.	Food, printed items, labor and décor can often be sourced locally.
REDUCED TOXICITY	Event supplies that use and release fewer harmful chemicals when compared to other products.	If you're using paper, look for process chlorine-free. Green-certified cleaners can also be requested.
CERTIFIED SUSTAINABLE	Has earned a third party stamp of approval.	Look for Forest Stewardship Council certified paper, USDA Organic food, Green Seal cleaners, and LEED®-certified venues and hotels, to name a few.
COOPERATIVES OR SOCIAL ENTERPRISES	You can do business with a traditional business, or one that improves human and environmental well-being as their primary goal.	Look for giveaways that are made by organizations that employ or train at-risk or vulnerable groups.

70. **Walk through venue to confirm accessible routes are clearly marked and have no obstructions.**

71. **Walk through exhibit hall to confirm sustainability compliance and donation stream.**
Strangest item seen left behind on a show floor with no future planning? Koi fish!

72. **Make sure hotel front desk staff informs guests of your event's sustainable practices.**
Provide the hotel with a simple list of things you would like to ensure they mention at check-in.

73. **Review sustainability practices during the pre-con.**

74. **Confirm no idling by delivery vehicles.**

75. **Brief onsite staff in sustainability practices.**
Prompting staff with small signs, prizes and messages to encourage recycling, less paper use and walking can keep best practices top-of-mind.

76. **Confirm onsite staff members are trained on waste management plans.**
This is especially important if you have made special arrangements for your event.

77. **Turn off AV and office equipment when not in use.**

78. **Conduct back of house tour.**
Look for waste sorting, food packaging, signage for health and safety, first aid kit, green team wall, and food donation.

79. **Confirm food is local by visiting the store room, refrigerators and kitchen.**
Look for delivery boxes that indicate where food has been shipped from.

80. **Check that green arrangements have been implemented such as bulk condiments, no disposable service ware and recycling bins in meeting rooms.**

81. **Remind registration team about green practices.**
Examples: Ask if participants want lanyards and conference bags and send reminders about name badge collection.

82. **Check that the hotel has undergone ECPAT (End Child Prostitution, Child Pornography and Trafficking of Children for Sexual Purposes) training for human trafficking prevention in the last 12 months.**
Human trafficking is a crime and human rights issue. It involves trading people for sexual slavery and compulsory, unpaid labor. Trafficking criminals may use hotels as a place to conduct business, so knowing how to spot signs is important.

FOR MORE INFORMATION ABOUT THE ECPAT CODE VISIT
www.thecode.org

BACK OF HOUSE TOUR

A key step in making sure that your planned initiatives take place is to conduct a back of house tour on arrival. Things to check include:

KITCHEN:

❏ Is food waste being composted or donated?

❏ Where is food being sourced? *(tip: check the produce boxes, they often say where produce is from)*

❏ Are proper food safety practices being followed?

❏ Are health inspection certificates on display?

HOUSEKEEPING DEPARTMENT:

❏ Are environmentally friendly cleaning products being used?

❏ Are staff members trained on the linen and towel reuse programs?

❏ Is waste being sorted for recycling on housekeeping carts?

❏ Do paper products contain recycled materials?

WORK AREAS:

❏ Is a first aid kit available?

❏ Are health and safety records displayed?

❏ Is there a Green Team bulletin board sharing staff sustainability initiatives?

LOADING DOCK:

❏ Are vehicles idling?

❏ Is waste being sorted into recycling, composting and landfill?

❏ How are they handling broken furniture, grease, wood pallets, plastic film and carpet?

ENDING SLAVERY AND HUMAN TRAFFICKING RELATED TO THE EVENT INDUSTRY

As meeting and event professionals, we have both an opportunity and a responsibility to help fight against slavery and human trafficking related to events and their supply chains. Human trafficking occurs in different ways in connection to the meetings and events industry. These include trafficking of adults and children for sexual exploitation as well as for labor (notably in the areas of construction, manufacturing, food production and housekeeping).

What to watch for in hotels

ECPAT-USA offers an e-learning module developed with the American Hotel and Lodging Association's Educational Institute that focuses on sex trafficking of children and offers specific advice on what housekeeping, lobby employees, security, and restaurant staff should be on the lookout for. Meeting professionals can also take the training and report their suspicions to hotel management and/or the police. Importantly, we can require that our hotels adopt The Tourism Child-Protection Code of Conduct, the travel industry's commitment to fight child trafficking, and train employees on what to do if they suspect a victim of trafficking is in their hotel property. For more information visit **www.thecode.org**.

WHAT TO WATCH FOR IN THE SUPPLY CHAIN

Two areas of concern related to slavery and human trafficking are **cocoa** and **seafood**.

COCOA: The cocoa industry has a long-standing record of forced child labor in the production of cocoa for chocolate in West Africa. Progress towards eradicating child labor in the production of cocoa has been slow and complicated. Fairly traded chocolate includes verification that the cocoa has been sourced free from forced child labor. For more information, visit **www.cocoainitiative.org**.

SEAFOOD: In March, 2015, the Associated Press released information on a year long investigation on slavery in the seafood industry. As part of the investigation, AP spoke to more than 40 current and former slaves in Benjina, Indonesia, and tracked and documented the transportation of a single large shipment of slave-caught seafood from the Indonesian village, to a harbor in Thailand where it was loaded onto trucks that were followed to dozens of factories, cold storage plants and the country's biggest fish market. The tainted seafood mixes in with other fish at several sites in Thailand, including processing plants. Official records show that several of those Thai factories ship to the US, Europe and Asia. For more information, visit **www.sustainablebrands.com/news_and_views/supply_chain/mike_ hower/ap_your_seafood_may_come_slaves**.

PART TWO:
PROGRAM ELEMENTS

 **Meeting Design**

 **Trade Shows, Fairs and Exhibitions**

 **Community Service Projects**

 **Participant Actions**

 **Share Your Story**

 **Sustainability-focused Sponsorship Opportunities**

 **Event Marketing**

83. **Re-evaluate if past practices now have better alternatives.**

84. **Plan room layouts for mobile accessibility devices.**
Don't forget to leave wide enough aisles and equal and convenient seating areas for participants with accessibility needs.

85. **Design the event program in consideration of participants with special needs.**
Examples include: Providing captioning, translation, assisted listening devices and sufficient lighting.

86. **Include sustainability topics and experts in the event program.**

87. **Prepare a budget that tracks sustainability savings and cost.**

88. **Design schedule with sufficient time for individuals to practice their wellness and faith activities.**

89. **Offer a virtual option to your participants.**
This can increase your audience and allow greater flexibility for attendees to meet their time, money and environmental needs.

90. **Select dates that don't conflict with religious holy days or festivals.**

91. **Use creative alternatives to encourage walking.**
Consider providing live entertainment along walking routes. To promote safety, recommend that participants walk in groups along the most direct and well-lit routes.

92. **Include questions about sustainability in the Call for Presentations.**

INTERFAITH CALENDAR
www.interfaithcalendar.org

BREAKING DOWN
PARTICIPATION
BARRIERS

As event designers, the choices that we make affect both the reality and the perception of inclusivity of our events. Here are a few easy ways that will start you on the path towards making your events more inclusive. An inclusive event is designed for all people to be able to fully participate, and embraces all forms of diversity, including ethnicity, age, gender, gender identity, disability, sexual orientation and religion. Inclusive events are also accessible, meaning that the services, facilities and program have been designed for people with disabilities to fully participate.

PLANNING:
- Ask your participants what they need to be fully included.
- Allocate budget funds or secure a sponsor for accessibility requirements.
- Seek out suppliers with experience working with diverse groups and audiences.

FACILITIES:
- Ask for verification of compliance with relevant accessibility regulations. For example in the US ask for verification of Americans with Disabilities Act (ADA) compliance.
- Ensure that all routes to, from and between event spaces are accessible and clearly marked, free of obstructions and direct.
- Personally inspect rooms, washrooms, elevators and other public spaces for accessibility considerations including ramps, door openers, wide doorways, sharps disposals, braille signage and easy to reach elevator buttons.

ROOM SETUPS:
- Provide space for mobility device users to circulate easily in the meeting space and accessible seating areas throughout the area with easy to reach electrical outlets.
- Ensure that lighting and sound levels are at the needed level for all forms of visual and auditory communication.
- Check that registration, front desk and other public use areas have lowered table heights.

COMMUNICATION:
- Offer materials in alternative formats such as large print, braille, captions or audio recorded.
- Offer sign-language interpretation, real-time captioning and assisted listening devices based on the needs and requests of the participants.
- In consultation with the user and sign-language interpreter, provide appropriate space, lighting and sight lines for interpretation.

SPEAKERS:

- Consider diversity in speaker selection.
- Include accessibility, diversity and inclusion as education topics.
- Provide accessible stages, lecterns and audiovisual equipment.

TRANSPORTATION:

- Ensure that there are sufficient accessible transportation options from arrival points to your event venue.
- Limit the need for transportation by selecting venues in close proximity to each other.
- Offer accessible transportation options between event venues.

FOOD AND BEVERAGE:

- Provide clearly-labeled food options to meet faith-based, medically-based and values-based needs.
- Minimize the use of buffets or provide stations that are designed for users of mobility devices.
- Develop strategies with your food service provider to avoid cross-contamination of allergens.

SCHEDULE:

- Select dates that don't conflict with dates of religious or cultural significance.
- Schedule meal times and provide space for participants to observe faith-based practices.
- Provide long breaks for the benefit of persons with disabilities to traverse between locations, nursing parents and service animal relief.

MARKETING:

- Select diverse images that are suitable to the audience and use colors that are not culturally offensive.
- As part of the registration forms, ask if the participant has accessibility-related needs.
- As part of the event evaluation, ask whether or not the facilities and the program met accessibility requirements.

RESOURCES:

- Provide information about mobility device rentals and accessible transportation providers in pre-event marketing and materials.
- Have information about outdoor areas and veterinarians for service animals readily available.
- Have information about places of worship readily available.

. . . .

**All of this is just a start to breaking down the barriers to participation.
For more information, see the following resources:**

- Office of the First Minister and Deputy First Minister - Event Planning – Access Checklist: Issues which may impact on people with disabilities. http://www.ofmdfmni.gov.uk/access_checklist_28_05_pdf.pdf
- US Department of Justice – Accessible Information Exchange: Meeting on a Level Playing Field http://www.ada.gov/business/accessiblemtg.htm
- US Department of Transportation – Checklist for Planning Accessible Meetings and Events http://www.dot.gov/citizens/disability/checklist-planning-accessible-meetings-and-events
- Council of Ontario Universities – Accessible Event & Conference Planning http://www.accessiblecampus.ca/aoda-everyday/reference-library/accessible-event-conference-planning/

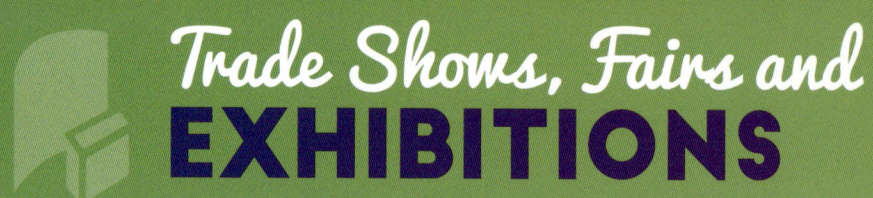

Trade Shows, Fairs and EXHIBITIONS

93. **Eliminate individual waste bins in exhibit booths, or ensure recycling is provided with them.**

94. **Ask exhibitors to reduce and reuse packaging and provide storage.**

95. **Provide central recycling stations.**
Don't forget your recycling stations might be different for set-up and tear-down when you may need to dispose of film plastic, graphics and carpet. During public hours you may only need simple recycling stations for participant paper, food and containers.

96. **Ask exhibitors not to bring handouts and offer lead retrieval.**
Advise them on accurate counts for necessary handouts.

97. **Provide exhibitor services kits digitally and request the general services contractor to prominently highlight sustainability options that are available.**

98. **Eliminate or reduce carpet or padding use where possible.**

99. **Require that exhibitor giveaways meet social and environmental criteria (see Sustainability Slang graphic).**

100. **Provide rewards and incentives to exhibitors for sustainability practices.**
Identify exhibitors that meet minimum guidelines with a special label. Include participating exhibitors in a draw for a free 10 x 10 booth, if space permits. Another thought: give Green Exhibitors free or discounted access to a virtual collateral rack.

101. **Educate booth staff about sustainability practices.**
Often the person buying a booth is not the one staffing it during the show.

102. **Provide exhibitors with information on your donation program and invite them to participate.**
Green stickers are an easy way for exhibitors to mark items they are leaving for donation, and can be handed out at the exhibitor services desk.

103. **Provide sustainable travel information to exhibitors.**

104. **Have exhibitors consolidate freight.**
Provide exhibitors with a list of recommended freight providers that have an environmental management program, such as SmartWay, and encourage them to consolidate shipments.

TRADE SHOW SUSTAINABILITY: THE DIFFERENCE IT MAKES[22]

Let's look at the footprint results from an actual 500 exhibitor, 50,000 participant tradeshow that implemented sustainability initiatives.

985
booth trash bins.

80% of the trash put in these bins can be recovered by using recycling and compost eco stations and back of house sorting.

4,659
square meters of graphics were used.

By choosing sustainable substrates that are reusable, recyclable, upcyclable or donatable, less than 9% of these graphics went to landfill.

32,609
meters of shrink wrap was used for freight.

Of this, the majority (1,450 lbs) was recovered and recycled.

3,785 litres
of propane was used for forklifts.

This was 100% offset as part of the 886 metric tons of onsite event emissions.

37,015 km
traveled by freight.

Local storage and consolidated shipping helped reduce the amount of travel.

17,577
square meters of carpet.

By reusing carpet, 40 metric tons of landfill were avoided.

105. Include a community service project as a part of your event.

106. Work with your CVB/DMO or service network to identify community events or projects with team-building experience.

Some host cities may have plug-and-play service projects that they have worked with before which you can take advantage of.

107. Create a service project that leverages participant skills.

Working with educators? Doctors? Computer engineers? Try to tie your group skills and interest to your service project, considering causes like literacy, health and wellness and technology innovation.

108. Schedule your project to not compete with other events.

This ensures all participants can enjoy the service project, while also maximizing potential benefit.

109. Ensure your project has lasting impact through long-term partnerships or coordination with a local organization that will continue the work.

110. Highlight the service project and group in your event program, sessions and/or exhibit hall.

111. Make your project relevant to your audience and aligned with the organization.

As an example, the Convention Industry Council supports Dress for Success at the CMP Conclave. This program provides resources to women in need who are entering or returning to the workplace and do not have professional clothing needed to interview for (and secure) jobs.

112. Include the project(s) and sponsors(s) in your social media.

SUPPORTING YOUR COMMUNITY

We Can Make the World a Better Place... Together

Clean the World has distributed 17 million bars of soap in 97 countries as of December 2014 thanks to partnerships with the hospitality community. | **www.cleantheworld.org**

....

Rock and Wrap it Up has recovered over 1 billion meals since 1991 thanks in part to hospitality and sporting event donors | **rockandwrapitup.org**

....

The Shade Tree provides over 100,000 nights of shelter each year to women and children in Southern Nevada and is a legacy project of IMEX America. Each year, participants donate time, money and materials to enhance the shelter. **www.theshadetree.org**

....

Food Runners relay enough food from events and restaurants in San Francisco to provide over 4,000 meals to those in need every day. | **www.foodrunners.org**

....

Frank Water's FreeFill program reduces plastic bottle waste by providing refillable bottles at events. Proceeds from bottle sales support clean water projects in developing countries. | **www.frankwater.com**

....

Stop Hunger Now hosts meal packaging events where 30-40 volunteers can pack 10,000 meals in an hour to feed the undernourished globally. | **www.stophungernow.org**

> **Three quarters of the meeting planners surveyed said their company included a CSR activity in their meetings and events last year.**
>
> *—2013 Corporate Social Responsibility Survey, Successful Meetings*

113. Ask participants to bring their own lanyard, mug, water bottle and shampoo.

114. Invite participants to opt-in to receive a lanyard, printed program, and conference bag on registration page.

115. Encourage your participants to shop locally by promoting local businesses through CVB/DMO program.

116. Include green travel tips in your confirmation email.
Remind participants to reduce printing and to unplug electronic devices at home too.

117. Ask participants to be energy-wise in their guest rooms by turning off lights, closing blinds and adjusting thermostats.

118. Educate participants about how to sort waste using signage and green ambassadors.

119. Include sustainability related questions in event evaluations.
Examples: a) Please select the sustainability initiatives that you participated in during the event: (recycling, brought my own mug, chose vegetarian options, used a mobile event application instead of a printed program, etc.) b) What sustainability initiatives would you like us to include in future events?

Make a DIFFERENCE!

Here are six simple choices you can make to influence participant behavior at your 1000-person, three-day conference:

Provide a remote live-stream option to attend the event.
SAVINGS: 110 metric tons (242,500 pounds) of carbon emissions for 500 remote viewers.[23]

Contract rooms at a green hotel with a linen reuse program.
SAVINGS: 15,142 litres (4,000 gallons) of water.[24]

Provide program in an app and only print it on demand.
SAVINGS: Up to two trees and 196,841 litres (52,000 gallons) of water.[25]

Provide reusable mugs and beverage refill stations
SAVINGS: 6,000 cups and 381 kg (840 pounds) of landfill from coffee drinkers alone.[26]

Design a Meatless Monday lunch.
SAVINGS: 2.83 metric tons carbon emissions, equal to the carbon sequestered by 72.6 seedlings grown for 10 years.[27]

Order chicken instead of beef for the gala dinner entrée.
SAVINGS: 1,257,584 litres (332,219 gallons), equal to half the volume of an Olympic-size swimming pool.[28]

120. **Showcase your sustainability features on buffets and menus.**
Include things like farmer names, distance from the venue, any organic or sustainability certifications and nutritional information.

121. **Have walk-in slides with environmental savings statistics or an infographic displayed as participants arrive in the general session room.**

122. **Include a sustainability section on the event's website.**
This can feature past sustainability reports, photos, actions for participants to take before the event, a list of your initiatives and details about your community service project.

123. **Submit articles or article topics to industry magazines profiling your sustainability success or community service project.**

124. **Create and share a case study.**
Your case study can be posted on your own website, shared with local colleges or universities for course work, or with an industry association to share with their members.

125. **Brief your official spokesperson on sustainability achievements.**
Provide them with fun facts that they can use in interviews with the media.

126. **Include sustainability in your social media strategy and consider a roving reporter.**
Send out information daily on what event participants have been able to accomplish.

127. **Issue a press release about your sustainability initiatives.**
Be sure to include a human interest aspect in the press release, and links for media to download photos.

128. **Apply for a sustainable event award.**
IMEX and GMIC offer annual sustainability awards. These are great case studies to learn about best practices.

129. **Have an onsite Sustainability Booth.**
Participants can learn about your initiatives, sign a pledge or ask questions at the booth.

130. **Give participants feedback about the difference their sustainable choices make.**

131. **Create a video showcasing your sustainable initiatives.**
This can be used at your closing event, to promote your event in the future, and/or as a teaching tool for college or university programs.

WATER SAVING TIPS
FOR MEETING PROFESSIONALS:[29]

Did you know?

 **1 SHEET OF PAPER= 10 LITRES**

 **1 CUP OF COFFEE= 130 LITRES**
Based on a 125 ml cup

 **1 COTTON TOTEBAG= 2,500 LITRES**
Based on a 250 g cotton totebag

**2 CUPS OF COFFEE +
1 TOTE BAG +
60 PAGES EACH**
 **X 750 PEOPLE** = **1 OLYMPIC SIZE SWIMMING POOL**

HOW TO REDUCE YOUR EVENT'S WATER FOOTPRINT

 FOOD
1. Reduce food waste.
2. Substitute or serve smaller portions of water intensive foods.
3. Reduce the demand for coffee with energetic speakers and programs.

 ACTIONS
1. Encourage short showers with a playlist of 4 minute power-shower songs.
2. Encourage participation in towel & linen reuse programs.
3. Add a legacy element to your event: hold a water crisis awareness program.

 MATERIALS
1. Have participants bring their own tote bags.
2. Book venues with well maintained water efficient equipment.
3. Go mobile! Replace printed event and exhibitor materials with an app.

 The amount of water required to produce 1 kg of meat is:
- 15,400 litres for beef
- 6,000 litres for pork
- 4,300 litres for chicken

 The average 8 minute shower uses **62 litres of hot water**
The average bath uses **80 litres of hot water**

 Water requirements for growing cotton vary around the globe.
- China: 6,000 litres/kg
- USA: 8,100 litres/kg
- India: 22,500 litres/kg

Sustainability Focused SPONSORSHIP OPPORTUNITIES

Sustainability initiatives are great not only for saving money through efficiency, but also for generating sponsorship revenues. Many organizations are interested in associating their brand with environmentally and socially responsible practices. Here are some ideas of sponsorship opportunities that can be offered:

132. **Reusable mugs and water bottles**

133. **Recycling program**

134. **Walking challenge**

135. **Solar or bike recharging stations**

136. **Water stations**

137. **Fairly-traded coffee or food experiences**

138. **Transit waiting room lounge**

139. **Bike share program**

140. **Green transportation program**

141. **Wellness area or program**

142. **Community service project**

143. **Virtual program or live-streaming**

144. **Badge back program**

145. **Shoe check (for comfortable walking shoes to business shoes)**

146. **Youth or student program**

147. **Green game that rewards people for sustainable actions**

148. **Scholarships**

149. **Alternative options to a conference bag**

150. **Green power**

151. **Carbon offset program**

Sustainable Event Sponsorship:
IT'S A WIN, WIN, WIN, WIN SITUATION

SPONSORS:

Gain marketing exposure and align their brand with sustainability.

MEETING ORGANIZERS:

Gain sponsorship revenue to offset costs and contribute to their bottom line.

PARTICIPANTS:

Gain an enhanced event experience.

PLANET:

Gains an improved environmental impact.

EXAMPLE: Sustainability Sponsorship In Action

DID YOU KNOW?

If 100 PARTICIPANTS

AT AN EVENT USE A REUSABLE WATER BOTTLE

enough energy could be saved to run an average American household for 200 HOURS

...not to mention 200 one-time use water bottles will be

DIVERTED FROM THE LANDFILL[30]

Event MARKETING

152. **Audit your lists before printing or mailing.**
Simply eliminating duplicates can reduce your printing and mailing costs significantly.

153. **Minimize print and make better paper choices.**
Examples include: Recycled content, double sided, vegetable inks, certified paper.

154. **Ensure graphics eliminate dates, cities, and any design elements that reduce reuse potential.**
If not possible on all signage, at least on the general directional signage that can be easily reused. Think "Lunch" or "Registration" signs. For non-reusable signs, select the most environmentally responsible option (see graphic).

155. **Produce an electronic conference program.**
If a printed program must be produced, adopt green design principles. This can involve reducing the size, number of pages or quantities printed. It can also mean using less white space and avoiding large blocks of colour and bleeds.

156. **Use a mobile event application to reduce signage and printing requirements.**

157. **Use a mail house for regional shipping to reduce individual long-haul mailings.**

RECYCLED CONTENT SAVES TREES! FIND OUT HOW MANY AT:

environmentalpaper.org

A "Sign" of SUSTAINABILITY?

Signs are essential to direct participants and establish your event brand. But what options are most sustainable? It depends on the situation! Use this handy table to help weigh the tradeoffs of common sign materials.

	What's it made of?	Green check	Caution	Commercial names
BOOTH AND KIOSK SIGNS				
Rigid PVC	Polyvinyl chloride (PVC) plastic, petroleum	Durable, highly reusable. May be recyclable by the manufacturer.	Processing can use harmful chemicals like mercury, lead, cadmium, phlathates. Difficult to recycle.	Komatex, Sintra
Fiberboard	Wood	Durable, reusable, renewable materials. May contain recycled content and be recyclable by the venue or manufacturer.	Processing can use harmful chemicals like formaldehyde.	HDF/MDF
Cardboard	Straw, paper, reeds	Renewable, recycled materials, light-weight. Lower relative energy footprint. Recyclable by venue.	Less durable than other alternatives.	Re-board, Falcon-Board, Freeman Honeycomb
FLEXIBLE BANNER SIGNS				
Vinyl	Polyvinyl chloride (PVC) plastic, petroleum	May contain recycled content or be biodegradable. Durable, reusable. May be recyclable by manufacturer. Can be upcycled into consumer goods, or donated.	Processing can use harmful chemicals like mercury, lead, cadmium, phlathates. Difficult to recycle.	
Stretch panel	Polyester	May contain recycled content. Durable, reusable, light-weight. May be recyclable by manufacturer. May be upcycled into consumer goods, or donated	Processing may involve chemical-heavy processes. Difficult to recycle.	
Paper	Wood, straw, grass	Renewable, recycled materials. Readily recyclable by venue.	Less durable than alternatives. Processing may use bleach.	
FREE-STANDING SIGNS				
Cardboard	Straw, paper, reeds	Renewable, recycled materials, light-weight. Recyclable by venue.		ReBoard, Falcon-Board, Freeman Honeycomb
Foamboard	Polystyrene, petroleum	Lower emissions and energy use than alternative. Lightweight. May be recyclable by manufacturer.	May use harmful chemicals like benzene in manufacture. Not recyclable by venue.	Ultra Board, Gator Board, foamcore

If you're using adhesive signs at your event beware! Most decal graphics are made of vinyl and can only be landfilled. They also may use high VoC glues. If you must use them, seek out water-bonded adhesives and recycled paper materials.

SIGNAGE OPTIONS [31]

	BOOTH CONSTRUCTION		FREE-STANDING SIGNS		BANNERS	
	Wood Fiberboard	Rigid PVC	Cardboard	Regular Foamboard	Banner Vinyl	Poplin Banner
Characteristics						
Weight (lbs./ft.2)	0.96	0.44	0.16	0.21	0.44	0.25
Lifespan	Very Long	Very Long	Medium	Medium	Long	Long
Manufacture						
Emissions-Chemicals	Some	Most	Least	Some	Most	Most
Emissions-CO_2	Some	Some	Least	Some	Most	Some
Raw Materials Used	Some	Most	Least	Most	Most	Most
Recycled Content	Some	Most	Some	Most	Most	Most
Chemicals Used	Some	Most	Least	Most	Most	Most
Chemicals Produced	Least	Most	Least	Most	Most	Some
Energy Consumption	Some	Some	Least	Some	Most	Most
Use						
Air Pollution	Some	Most	Least	Least	Some	Least
Leaching	Some	Most	Least	Most	Most	Most
Disposal						
Recyclable	Most	Most	Least	Most	Most	Most
Biodegradable	Least	Most	Least	Least	Most	Most
Compostable	Least	Most	Least	Most	Most	Most
Landfill	Least	Most	Least	Most	Most	Most
Leaching	Most	Most	Least	Most	Most	Least

Environmental Ranking

Least Concern   Some Concern   Most Concern

PART THREE:

THE NEXT STEPS

 **Sustainability Strategy**

158. **Create a green team with staff and vendors who can help you identify opportunities and solutions.**

159. **Develop a sustainability policy (see graphic).**

160. **Pick an issue to prioritize and set a goal.**
Start with something you care about, like food waste, or a project that gives back to the community.

161. **Build and share the business case.**
We practice event sustainability because it's the right thing to do, and it also makes business sense! Keep track of how your efforts contribute to your organization through press articles, customer feedback and cost reductions. The business case can include reputational gains, image building and risk reduction.

162. **Include your sustainability intentions and/or policy in your RFP and consider vendor responses when making selection decisions.**

163. **Dig deeper to find out where your suppliers source their goods and services.**
Keep asking them and they, in turn, will continue to ask their suppliers.

164. **Think about how you will consistently measure the outcome of sustainability program.**

165. **Require and verify proof of sustainability claims.**
Greenwashing, or over-stating environmental benefits of products and services, is a risk you want to avoid. So ask suppliers for proof of practice.

166. **Include sustainability expectations and consequences in contracts.**
List expectations in agreements, including any incentives or consequences.

167. **Include sustainability results in post event reports.**

RECIPE FOR
an Event Sustainability Policy

Prep: Check for ISSUES
Before writing your policy it's a good idea to check the cupboards for event sustainability problems that might be hanging around. For example, does your event generate a lot of waste? Or take place in a sensitive outdoor environment? Shape your policy to address your unique opportunities and challenges.

Assemble 1 part VALUES
List principles that convey the big-picture intentions of your policy. Think single words that are clearly understood that convey the spirit of what you want to accomplish. Examples include: Inclusivity, Stewardship, Transparency, and Leadership.

Mix in 3 parts GOALS
Your policy will need specific objectives that are measurable, achievable and realistic. This might include: Reducing solid waste, enhancing participant experiences, or providing local community benefit. Focus on simple verb-object statements that you can control and measure outcomes for.

Bake using the following TOOLS
While your policy can be a short one to two page document of commitments, it is implemented in a variety of ways. Act on your policy by:

❑ Including it in tenders and contracts.

❑ Adding it to employee hiring and reviews.

❑ Reflecting it in any speaker, exhibitor or participant codes of conduct.

❑ Integrating it with event communications and social media.

ENDNOTES

1   Webber, C.L. and Matthews, H.S. (2008) Food Miles and the Relative Climate Impacts of Food Choices in the United States. Environmental Science and Technology, 42 (10) 3508-3513.

2   Doyle, A. (February 19, 2013). U.N. offers banquet of blemished food to highlight waste. Reuters. Retrieved December 16, 2014 from: http://www.reuters.com/article/2013/02/19/us-food-waste-id US-BRE91I0YT20130219

3   Water Footprint Network. Product Water Footprints: Animal Products. Retrieved March 23, 2015 from: http://www.waterfootprint.org/?page=files/Animal-products

4   Food and Agriculture Organization. Reduction of bycatch and discards. Retrieved April 23, 2015 from: http://www.fao.org/fishery/topic/14832/en

5   World Wildlife Federation. Threats. Overfishing. Retrieved April 23, 2015 from: https://www.worldwildlife.org/threats/overfishing

6   Chefs Collaborative. Trash Fish Dinners. Retrieved April 23, 2015 from: http://www.chefscollaborative.org/programs/seafood-solutions/trash- fish-dinners/

7   Nordic Choice Hotels. Food Waste. Retrieved February 27, 2015 from: https://www.nordicchoicehotels.com/social-responsibility-in-nordic-choice-hotels/the-food-revolution/matavfall/

8   Carbon Clear. Disposable Cups vs. Reusable Cups Solving the Carbon Intensity Question. Retrieved April 23, 2015 from: http://www.carbon-clear.com/files/cup_assessment.pdf

9   Strand, O. (February 7, 2012). With coffee, the price of individualism can be high. New York Times. Retrieved December 17, 2014 from: http://www.nytimes.com/2012/02/08/dining/single-serve-coffee-brewers-make-convenience-costly.html?_r=0

10 Clean the World. FAQ. Retrieved April 28, 2015 from: https://cleantheworld.org/about-us/faq/

11 MeetGreen. Aggregate Data from 2007–2014.

12 MeetGreen. Event-specific waste audits from 2014.

13 Gunders, D. (August, 2012). Wasted: How America Is Losing Up to 40 Percent of Its Food from Farm to Fork to Landfill National Resources Defense Council. Retrieved April 23, 2015 from: http://www.nrdc.org/food/files/wasted-food-ip.pdf

14 Carpet Recovery America Effort. Yardage Calculator. Retrieved April 23, 2015 from: https://carpetrecovery.org/recovery-effort/yardage-calculator/

15 United States Environmental Protection Agency. Communicating the Benefits of Recycling. Retrieved April 23, 2015 from: http://www.epa.gov/osw/conserve/tools/localgov/benefits/

16 Rock and Wrap it Up! Food Recovery Calculator. App by Eventmobi. Retrieved April 24, 2015 from: http://eventmobi.com/rwu1/

17 Bay Area Rapid Transit. Carbon Calculator. Retrieved December 17, 2014 from: http://www.bart.gov/guide/carbon

18 Leicester County Council. Calculating our carbon footprint. Retrieved April 28, 2015 from: http://www.leics.gov.uk/calculating_our_carbon_footprint.pdf

19 Chestney, N. (December 12, 2012) London Olympics' emissions 28 percent lower than forecast - organisers Reuters. Retrieved on April 23, 2015 from: http://uk.reuters.com/article/2012/12/12/uk-olympics-emissions-idUKBRE8BB0C820121212

20 MeetGreen. Corporate Sustainability Report. Retrieved April 24, 2015 from: http://meetgreen.com/about/corporate-sustainability-report/

ENDNOTES

21 Calculated using Environmental Reporting – Guidelines for Company Reporting on GHG Emissions, DEFRA, UK as listed in GHG Protocol - Mobile Guide v1.3. (03/21/05) Retrieved April 24, 2015 from: http://www.ghgprotocol.org/files/ghgp/tools/co2-mobile.pdf

22 MeetGreen data from an actual 500-exhibitor tradeshow as provided by Freeman.

23 MeetGreen sample hybrid event analysis (unpublished).

24 Calculated based on Rogers, R. Reusing Hotel Towels: The Nitty Gritty. Stanford Alumni Magazine. Retrieved on January 28, 2015 from: https://alumni.stanford.edu/get/page/magazine/article/?article_id=29072

25 Calculated assuming a 40 page printed program using Murthy, P., & Smith, C. L. (2010). "Water Availability". Women's global health and human rights. Sudbury, Mass: Jones and Bartlett Publishers. Page 445.

26 Calculated based on two cups per day and 16 oz paper cups with lids.

27 Calculated using 4 oz servings of beef vs. 4 oz tofu or beans. Environmental Working Group. Meat-eater's Guide to Climate Change and Health. Retrieved January 28, 2015 from http://static.ewg.org/reports/2011/meateaters/pdf/report_ewg_meat_eaters_guide_to_health_and_climate_2011.pdf?_ga=1.1609329.1563467288.1426871905 p. 6. Carbon sequestration figure calculated based on U.S. Environmental Protection Agency. Greenhouse Gas Equivalencies Calculator. Retrieved April 28, 2015 from: http://www.epa.gov/cleanenergy/energy-resources/calculator.html#results

28 Calculated based on approximately 4 oz servings using data from Waterfootprint.org. Product Gallery. Retrieved on April 24, 2015 from: http://www.waterfootprint.org/?page=files/productgallery

29 Calculated using cotton, coffee and meat statistics from Waterfootprint.org. Product Gallery. Retrieved on April 24, 2015 from: http://www.waterfootprint.org/?page=files/productgallery; bath and shower statistics from Kivner, M. (22 November, 2011) People's showering habits revealed in survey. BBC News. Retrieved April 24, 2015 from: www.bbc.co.uk/news/science-environment-15836433; and paper statistics from ONEDROP Foundation. World Water Day. Retrieved April 24, 2015 from: www.onedrop.org/en/projects/projects-overview/WorldWaterDay.aspx

30 Calculated using water bottle energy statistics from P.H. Gleick, P.H. and Cooley, H.S. (19 Feb 2009) Energy Implications of Bottled Water. Environmental Research Letters accessed April 24, 2015 from: http://iopscience.iop.org/1748-9326/4/1/014009/pdf/erl9_1_014009.pdf and average American household energy use from US Energy Information Administration accessed April 24, 2015 from: http://www.eia.gov/tools/faqs/faq.cfm?id=97&t=3

31 MeetGreen Research, compiled by Elliott, A. (2014).